CONTENTS

THE PAST

The best player in the National Basketball Association did not come by his toughness casually. Allen Iverson, born to a 15-year-old unwed mother and an 18-year-old absentee father, grew up in low-income projects in Newport News or "Bad News," Va. as the locals called it, and later in Hampton, Va., for a time in a two-bedroom dwelling that smelled of raw sewage after a pipe that ran under the building ruptured and the public service company never repaired it properly.

Often, there was no power and no heat because his mother Ann couldn't afford to pay the bills. Just as often, young Allen would stay home, taking care of his baby sister Liesha, who had suffered seizures since birth, while his mother worked at the shipyards or at a clothing factory.

"There were times when Allen never knew where his next meal was going to be," Iverson's basketball coach at Bethel High, Mike Bailey, told the *Washington Post*. "Here's a kid who couldn't take a bath because he had no running water because it had been turned off."

Iverson shrugs. "Everybody in my family struggled," he said. "It was nothing new, the lights being cut off or anything. I mean, it was something I had been dealing with my whole life."

As a child, he often promised Ann he would buy her a red Jaguar.

"I knew I had to succeed for them," Iverson told *Sports Illustrated* in 1998.

"People would say, 'Man, that's a million-to-one shot to make it to the NBA,' but I'd say, 'Not for me it ain't,' because if I didn't succeed, well, I don't wanna think about it. I thought, for all the suffering they've done, they need me to make it. They ought to have some satisfaction in life."

Allen's real father, Allen Broughton, had little contact with his son throughout his young life and is currently in the third year of a nine-year sentence for pleading guilty to stabbing his former girlfriend. His surrogate father, Michael Freeman, served 22 months in the state prison after being convicted of drug possession with the intent to distribute, and later served 23 months for violating his parole. In 1997, he was sent back to jail for another parole violation. Another father figure was killed.

Allen was no stranger to violence. During one summer, eight of his friends were killed by violent means. In high school, he attended a party at a hotel

> "It was nothing new, the lights being cut off or anything. I mean, it was something I had been dealing with my whole life."

Opposite: "I knew I had to succeed for them"—Iverson celebrates his MVP honors with his mother Ann.

Georgetown University coach John Thompson

Opposite: Iverson's need to support his family meant his time as a Hoya was cut short.

where a man was shot to death. But jail was an experience Allen never suspected he would learn about firsthand.

"I'm not a person who walks down the street and wants to be part of violence," Iverson said in the fall of 2000. "There are people like that, but I don't live that way. I want more out of life."

Nevertheless, on Valentine's Day 1993, in his junior year in high school, Iverson was involved in an event that would change his life.

Some witnesses in that summer's two-day trial in Hampton circuit court testified that Iverson began the altercation at the Circle Lanes bowling center, when he began swearing at a 22-year-old white man and his friends for no reason.

One prosecution witness said suddenly someone hit him from behind and a melee ensued with chair throwing and fists flying. One employee of the bowling center and a high school classmate of Iverson's, said that he saw Iverson hit a woman and knock her out with a chair and that Iverson later hit him as well.

Iverson, however, offered a much different version, saying one of the white men involved started the riot by hurling racial epithets at him and then hitting Iverson with a chair. Iverson said further that a friend pulled him away and that he left the building as the brawl broke out.

No question, the trial affected his standing in the college basketball community, though not so much that he was un-recruitable. One assistant coach from a major college attended his trial. Another visited him at the minimum-security work farm, where he ended up serving four months on a conviction on three felony counts—later overturned—for "maiming by mob." Still another told his hometown paper, "Unless he's behind bars, we're recruiting him. It's as simple as that."

The town and state were racially divided. Around Hampton, his supporters wore "Free Iverson" t-shirts and graffiti on buildings read "Free Bubbachuck," while in another part of town, a scarecrow wearing Iverson's jersey was hung in effigy.

The exploits of "Bubbachuck," (a combination of Iverson's uncles' names) as he is called by family and friends, are legendary, as the Virginia Player of the Year in two sports scored 37 points that year in Bethel High's basketball season opener just three days after the state title football game in which he threw for 201 yards, returned a punt for a 60-yard touchdown and intercepted two passes.

The summer before, Iverson had become a sudden sensation when he was named MVP at five different basketball tournaments and already, basketball experts were comparing him to established NBA stars.

"I always figured I was going to go to one of those big football schools, Florida State, Notre Dame," Iverson said in a 1996 interview with *Sports Illustrated*. "Football was my first love. Still is...I didn't even want to play basketball at first. I thought it was soft. My mother's the one who made me go to tryouts. I thank her forever. I came back and said, 'I like basketball too."

Iverson said after the trouble started, it was the basketball schools that stayed interested in him. Though he had no criminal record, he had originally

Above: The number one pick in the 1996 NBA draft.

Right: The skills Iverson showed at Georgetown made him irresistible to the Sixers.

been sentenced to five years in prison before being granted "conditional clemency" by outgoing Virginia Governor L. Douglas Wilder, the condition being that he not play organized sports until he graduated from high school.

Two years later, the conviction was overturned and Iverson's record expunged by the state court of appeals due to insufficient evidence.

"I had to use the whole jail situation as something positive," he told the *Los Angeles Times* in 1996. "I knew when I got out that my back was against the wall and that just made me work that much harder, knowing that everybody thought it was over for me.

"I always knew that I still had to take care of my family, even though I was coming out of jail. And I just tried to learn from everything that I witnessed while I was incarcerated. I found out a lot about people and who they are and how people do things. And I found out a lot about myself, let me know how strong I was."

In jail, he shot at a netless rim to keep sharp. "I had a bigger picture for life," he said. "I wasn't going to go back to the sewer."

After Ann Iverson implored Georgetown University coach John Thompson to take a look at her son, he finally agreed after meeting and talking with Allen, assuring him he would receive no extra sympathy from him.

Still, Georgetown was perfect for Iverson, with Thompson shielding his players naturally and taking special care of his stars. Iverson wasn't allowed his first interview until three months into the season and he wasn't available for any one-on-one chats with the media. After the game, reporters could ask him questions but were told emphatically that they were only to be on the subject of basketball. A Georgetown official timed his interviews and monitored them, lest a reporter wandered from the subject.

Still, he couldn't be shielded from everything. Opposing fans chanted "Jailbird," at him and in Philadelphia, ironically, when Georgetown played Villanova, there hung the sign, "Go Bowling, Go to Jail, Go to Georgetown."

In his first college exhibition game, Iverson scored 36 points in 23 minutes. But his first regular-season game as a collegian, against top-ranked Arkansas, was less than impressive as he shot 27 percent in a 19-point performance. "He's got no feel for the game," said one of the commentators.

Still, there was something there and that something was obvious. "I've seen three calf shows, nine horse ropings, I even saw Elvis once," said Arkansas coach Nolan Richardson. "But I've never seen a guard do what he can do with the basketball."

After two years at Georgetown, Iverson told his coach, who had never seen a player leave before his senior year, that he had to turn pro to support his family. "Every time I came home, it seemed like their living situation got worse," Iverson explained. And on June 26, 1996, he was the first player chosen in the NBA draft.

His rookie contract with the Philadelphia 76ers—three years for $9.4 million. His first purchase—a red Jaguar for his mother.

"I've been through so many obstacles that I feel, you know, I deserve to be picked number one," Iverson said at the draft. "I want to start my own era. I think my era has come."

 # THE IMAGE

Misunderstood. Allen Iverson has told his mother it is the one word he wants engraved in his tombstone. He is right, of course. Everything about Iverson is misunderstood, though it would take a lengthy analysis to figure out exactly how.

Is he really, for example, a conservative, buttoned-down gentleman beneath the cornrows and do-rag, tattoos and baggy clothes?

No way Iverson would agree to that. And everything he does and says suggests that he wants to be understood perfectly. Still, chronicling the life and times of Allen Iverson is to see a host of contradictions. One thing is clear—Iverson can't seem to avoid controversy, no matter how hard he may try.

Iverson's tattoos and cornrows paint an image of him that seems to enflame some people, just on face value alone.

"Allen is a target because he's very visible and he's very different," Lenny Wilkens, the winningest coach in NBA history, told the *Philadelphia Inquirer*. "It doesn't give people the right to make racial remarks to him. Sometimes, we are in the spotlight and we have to be careful about what we say. But he's a young guy and it's not so much about being macho, it's just that you get tired of people saying things to you."

Iverson's coach at Georgetown, John Thompson, said Iverson was often a target of verbal abuse, even from the parents of his own teammates in college.

"Parents who, selfishly, didn't like the number of shots he was taking or how he was playing," said Thompson, who lauded Iverson and his mother for not responding and still rooting for those players. "Allen has got to be careful controlling himself because he's been taking it for a long, long time," said Thompson. "But it comes to a point in everybody's life when you get a little fed up."

> "Allen has got to be careful controlling himself because he's been taking it for a long, long time," said Thompson. "But it comes to a point in everybody's life when you get a little fed up."

One recent example came in February, 2001 when, after his MVP All-Star game performance and just as things were going as well as they had ever been off the court, a nationally televised game pitting Iverson's Philadelphia 76ers against the Indiana Pacers brought trouble again.

On camera, Iverson was heard using profanity toward a fan, and was seen wagging his tongue at another, bringing some strong criticism from the commentators calling the game.

What the microphones did not pick up, Iverson and his teammates said later, was a barrage of insults and racial slurs that Iverson said pushed him to the breaking point.

Sixers guard Eric Snow said he was shocked. "Everything was being said to him, I mean everything," said Snow. "Just think of it and it was being said. Some old lady was saying something to him. Another was a teenager. It was vicious."

Part of Iverson's problem in the NBA is those he associates with, childhood friends, his "posse" in his terms, his "entourage" to others.

Other times, he simply allows himself to be in situations that cry poor judgment. In August 1997 Iverson was arrested for gun possession and cited for possession of marijuana while a passenger in his own car with someone he claimed to have barely known. Iverson later received three years probation.

> **Sixers guard Eric Snow said he was shocked. "Everything was being said to him, I mean everything," said Snow. "Just think of it and it was being said. Some old lady was saying something to him. Another was a teenager. It was vicious."**

Previous pages: Iverson showed quickly that he belonged in the NBA.

Opposite: Iverson had much to shout about during the 2001 playoffs.

Left: With teammate Eric Snow.

"Allen's a role model," Sixers former team president Pat Croce said at the time of Iverson's arrest. "Whether he did it or not, to be in that position is just unacceptable."

Less than a year later, Iverson's car was confiscated in a police dragnet when two of his longtime friends who were driving it at the time were caught in a drug deal. Iverson was not charged in that case.

Shortly after Iverson arrived in Philadelphia, Croce worried that his associations would be a problem and tried to intervene. "I told [some of them] 'You get in any trouble that reflects on Allen or me, I'll burn your houses down.' I can talk trash with the best of them," said Croce, who, like Iverson, did much of his growing up on the streets. "But if I was in a different city at the age of 21, I'd surround myself with my family and my best friends too.

"They're the only ones he can trust now that he's got a bunch of bucks..."

And Iverson is not likely to drop his buddies. "A lot of people in this world have friends, but they look at my friends a lot tougher than they would look at anybody else's friends. I think it's unfair."

And then there's his hair. Iverson is proud of his cornrows, a symbol, no doubt, that he is different than the corporate suits who pay to watch him, and that he has more in common with the kids in the street, kids who are closer to his own age.

But even in his home arena, Iverson hears taunts about his hair, which he can't understand. "I got rows, but that don't mean I'm no gangbanger," he told *Sports Illustrated*. "I ain't never been in a gang. Why do people wanna judge me like that?"

The NBA has consistently gotten on Iverson, complaining that he does not conform to their uniform standards, that his black ankle braces cover up too much of his white socks, that his shorts are too long and that he should not have worn a white skull cap to receive his 1996–97 Rookie of the Year award.

Once recently, the league went so far as to airbrush Iverson's tattoos out of a cover photo on the NBA's *Hoop* Magazine.

"Damn, these people want me to wear Italian suits all the time like Michael [Jordan], want me to act like I'm 25, 26 or 27 years old," Iverson told *Sports Illustrated*. "Well, I'm not that old yet. I'm only 22. Don't rush me."

Still, even his former agent tried to explain to Iverson that how he looked affected the way people thought of him, whether he liked it or not, and that that perception could end up hurting Iverson financially in the long run.

"If I walk into a bank and try to make a $500,000 deal for him and he comes in wearing his 'do rag, the white guys who run the bank are going to think he's there to rob the place, not sign a deal," said David Falk. "So, if it's important for him to make the statement as opposed to signing the deal, that's fine, as long as he knows."

In one *Sports Illustrated* article in 1998, the author describes Iverson getting dressed after a game, slipping on one diamond and gold watch of 130 carats worth about $80,000; a 120-carat gold and diamond gold bracelet; diamond earrings of 3.5 carats each; and two gold and diamond necklaces—one with a diamond medallion in the shape of handcuffs. "To remind me," he said, "of where I never want to go back."

"You get in any trouble that reflects on Allen or me, I'll burn your houses down.' I can talk trash with the best of them. But if I was in a different city at the age of 21, I'd surround myself with my family and my best friends too."

Above: Pat Croce, Philadelphia's former team president.

Opposite: Iverson gives some love back.

19

Above: Iverson answers back.

Later, however, Iverson had to make people think when he explained his perspective. "People see someone with a lot of jewelry on, they go, 'He's a drug dealer, he doin' somethin' illegal,'" he said. "But they don't have to look at me like that. When I was little, my mom and I used to sit in the dark and talk about jewelry—all the cool jewelry we were gonna have someday. I told her, 'I'm gonna buy you the best jewelry in the world.' I think black people deserve things like that. I think my mom deserves it."

Indeed, not everything is as it appears. Iverson had two bodyguards at one time, for example, which people assumed were part of his "posse." In reality, he felt he needed them for protection.

And though he appears to be a free spirit, the father of two children, Tiaura, 6, and Deuce, 4, with wife Tawanna Turner, is also financially responsible for his mother, surrogate father, two sisters, his aunt and her three kids, and two uncles.

Iverson has shown great understanding, like the time when Croce's brother John, then the team's conditioning coach, was caught stealing money from Iverson's pants pocket in April of 2001. "It's nothing," Iverson told a mortified Croce, saying there was no need to apologize. "It's only family."

But Iverson has also appeared thoughtless, like the time he caught the wrath of friend and supporter Magic Johnson when he failed to show up for Johnson's charity game in L.A. after promising to attend. Iverson admitted to staying out too late the night before and missing his flight, thus effectively ending the friendship.

Iverson has also, at times, infuriated teammates by being late to practice or missing weight training sessions.

Iverson often acts as if he doesn't care what the public, or the media, thinks of him, answering questions in a quiet monotone. His friends, however, say he's very funny in private, drawing humorous caricatures and talking incessantly. They also point out his charity work and frequent visits to hospitals, which he will not allow the team to publicize.

During the 2001 NBA Finals, Pat Covas, an assistant principal at Iverson's high school who was also the basketball team trainer, told the *Philadelphia Inquirer* that Iverson has "two sides. When he's out, when he's with his boys, he's a hip-hop man," said Covas. "When he's with older people, he's kind, quiet, polite and speaks the Queen's English."

In a March 1998 interview with the *Philadelphia Daily News*, Iverson said he only cares about his young fans. "Kids accept me," he said. "Everybody's not going to love me no matter what. I can't satisfy everybody. I don't try to get in trouble. I don't try to get bad press."

At times, Iverson has tried to conform. During the 1998 playoffs, he seemed to gladly adhere to coach Larry Brown's dress code, wearing suits to post-game press conferences during the playoffs.

But by early the next season, Iverson was once again bucking the establishment, in this case the establishment being Brown, saying, "I'm not going to let anybody tell me what to wear. I'll wear what I want. If [the Sixers] want to fine me for that, so be it."

Later, his mother told a reporter that her son hated wearing a suit and tie because it reminded him of the criminal trial he endured as a teenager.

In the final analysis, Iverson has been consistent about one thing and that's a realistic attitude about how he is perceived.

"I know there are people out there who don't like me, I know that," he said in 1999. "When I say there are a million people who love me and a million who hate me, I mean that everybody's not going to like you. Look at Jesus Christ. But once you accept the reality of that, it's easy to deal with everything else."

But as he said just last year, Iverson seems to understand that even supporters' patience wears thin eventually. "Mistakes happen," he said. "But after a while, you've got to stop making them twice."

And by the time the Sixers were ready to take on the Los Angeles Lakers for the NBA title, on the day of his 26th birthday, Iverson seemed to have figured it out.

"For the first time in my life, I'm conducting myself on and off the court like a professional," he said. "And it just took some growing up, you know? I'm 26 years old and I feel like I've done a lot of growing, just learning from my mistakes, just being human and trying to get better. All year I was just trying to make sure I set a good example for my teammates so they could follow someone that was trying to do everything the right way.

"That's what I was doing all season and that's what I'll continue to do, continue to try to keep growing as a man."

> "When I say there are a million people who love me and a million who hate me, I mean that everybody's not going to like you. Look at Jesus Christ. But once you accept the reality of that, it's easy to deal with everything else."

ALLEN AND LARRY

It was only a few seemingly harmless words uttered at the 2001 NBA All-Star game, as Commissioner David Stern handed Allen Iverson his Most Valuable Player award.

"Where's my coach?" Iverson asked, frantically looking around. "Where's coach Brown?"

And with that, the ice had seemingly melted for good.

Only a few seemingly harmless words, but in the public's perception, one of the most infamous and tempestuous player-coach feuds in the history of professional sports appeared to be over.

That, of course, remains to be seen. Especially when you consider the history involved. But by the time of the 2001 NBA Finals between the 76ers and Lakers, Philadelphia coach Larry Brown seemed to have gained perspective on his stormy relationship with his star player.

"Maybe I didn't give it enough thought or time to understand what this kid's about, and that's been the neatest thing about my [improved] relationship with him," Brown said. "He doesn't always do it the way I would expect, or sometimes like, but I know where his heart is, and I think the reward is the fact that I'm sitting here talking to you about us being in the NBA Finals.

"It's because of what he's about. The kid has great character, and he cares about people that he trusts and knows have his best interests at heart."

If only Brown had understood that before.

And if only Iverson had learned when to keep his mouth shut.

When Brown took over the Sixers in 1997, signing a five-year, $30 million contract, he inherited the NBA's resident juvenile delinquent, a selfish player who never saw a shot he could pass up, treated defense like a bad habit and who did not like people telling him what to do.

In some ways, he inherited an individual not unlike himself. Both men grew up without many advantages in life—Iverson in the projects of Hampton, Va., and Brown in an apartment over a bakery and usually without heat in a tough Jewish and black neighborhood in New York.

> "He doesn't always do it the way I would expect, or sometimes like, but I know where his heart is, and I think the reward is the fact that I'm sitting here talking to you about us being in the NBA Finals."

Opposite: Coach and Captain converse during the NBA Finals.

Above: The improved relationship between Iverson and Brown was clear to see in 2000–2001.

Iverson's real father was in jail, as was his surrogate father. Brown's father died of a heart attack, but six-year-old Larry did not learn about the death until more than a month after it happened because his mother was afraid of how he would take the news.

Brown, at 5-foot-8, played with reckless abandon and had a temper as a player, once getting kicked out of Atlantic Coast Conference play in college for punching an opposing player.

Both Brown and Iverson had always been overly sensitive, often temperamental and moody. It killed Brown, who holds the American Basketball Association single-game assists record, that he couldn't get Iverson to appreciate the fine art of passing. It annoyed Iverson that Brown didn't seem to appreciate his talents.

Iverson doesn't take public criticism well and he has never accepted coming out of a game—two issues that continually caused tension between he and Brown.

As grown men, both had two small children of the same ages and lived in mansions on the outskirts of Philadelphia, very close to each other. And yet, they were miles and miles apart.

Brown initially protected Iverson, but the stern taskmaster who learned at North Carolina at the feet of legendary coaches like Frank McGuire and Dean Smith that the team always comes first, grew quickly impatient.

One day, Brown made an excuse for one of Iverson's transgressions, telling one of his teammates that the kid, meaning Iverson, had a pretty tough childhood. The player responded, "Well, 12 guys in that locker room could probably say the same."

Brown agreed, and changed his approach.

24

Iverson doesn't take public criticism well and he has never accepted coming out of a game—two issues that continually caused tension between he and Brown.

In December 1999, Iverson blew up at Brown for taking him out of a game—along with his other four starters—for its final 20 minutes, 15 seconds, daring Brown to trade him, sarcastically mimicking him for benching him and saying he had no intention of staying in Philadelphia if another benching like that occurred.

"If I'm hurting this team, if my style of basketball is hurting this team, I need to get the hell out of here," Iverson said afterward.

In another game in April 1999, Iverson was 0-for-7 in the first quarter, including an ill-advised three-pointer to end the quarter, then was benched for the first two minutes, three seconds in the second. When Brown beckoned Iverson back into the game, he responded, "It's about time you put me back in."

Brown responded by pulling him back out for the rest of the game. Iverson told a teammate he was going to get dressed and leave before being persuaded otherwise, didn't join the team for half-time warm-ups and didn't come back to the bench until the second half began.

Afterward, Iverson said he was taking himself out of the lineup indefinitely because of a bruised thigh.

Brown said he resented that Iverson seemed to turn everything into "me-against-them." He warned Iverson that he would "face the consequences" if he chose not to follow team rules. At that point, team sources told reporters

Above: Coach Brown and Iverson plot their next move during the NBA Finals.

Brown said he resented that Iverson seemed to turn everything into "me-against-them." He warned Iverson that he would "face the consequences" if he chose not to follow team rules.

25

that Iverson was late to approximately 50 practices, not counting those he simply skipped, and constantly missed weight-training sessions, instead hiding in the bathroom with a bagful of tacos.

And Iverson constantly butted heads with Brown over the team dress code, even when he was seemingly complying with it.

Once, in the '99-'00 playoffs, after Brown required suits and ties, Iverson walked into the lockerroom in a designer ensemble. "See how good you look?" said Brown. Iverson, reported *Sports Illustrated*, then took the suit off and left it in a ball on the floor.

Later, they apparently made up, though the *Philadelphia Inquirer* reported that Brown had thought about retiring after the incident.

According to the *Inquirer*, Brown told Iverson, "I don't know if we can go on like this. If we don't fix this situation, I'm going to have to resign." Iverson reportedly talked Brown out of it, saying, "Coach, we're in this together. Neither of us are going anywhere."

Later Brown said, "Every coach has some problems, but it's no big deal...I love Allen. I want him here and I want to be here with him."

Said Iverson: "I don't know anything about him resigning or anything like that, but we did get in an argument and I was out of line. I called him and apologized for the way I spoke to him right after that because I felt bad. And I just came out and told him, 'I don't want you going anywhere. We're in this together and we're going to win [a championship] together. I'm in this all the way with you, coach. That's the way it's going to be.'"

And that's the way it seemingly always was between the two—love and hate.

And the Sixers were not blameless in the whole thing.

Once, during the 1999–2000 season, one night before Iverson returned from the injured list after missing ten games with a fractured right thumb, he showed up at the team hotel in New York declaring himself fit to play. He had not practiced the day before, did not travel with the team to New York and did not show up for the shootaround the morning of the game.

But instead of telling Iverson he would not be allowed to play because of that, the Sixers played games with the media and with Iverson, telling him they had forgotten his No. 3 jersey in Philadelphia, even though they, in fact, had it with them.

Brown said he told general manager Billy King that Iverson would not be allowed to play. Still, it was Brown who told reporters that it was because of Iverson's missing jersey that he did not play that night.

King said he was joking when he told Iverson the jersey was missing.

Clearly, it was a problem from the bottom up. "It would be a lot easier if I didn't have the issue," said then team president Pat Croce in the summer of 2000 about the Brown-Iverson rift. "I just wish it would be resolved. I always love it when they hug each other at the end of winning a game because then I can sit in the stands and breathe a sigh of relief."

Croce describes Brown and Iverson as "a 60-year-old coach who knows the world of basketball and a 26-year-old who knows the neighborhood of basketball. And the two have to mesh. I just have to be the referee once in a while."

Croce had to intervene again in the summer of 2000, following talk of a trade

Croce has described Brown and Iverson as "a 60-year-old coach who knows the world of basketball and a 26-year-old who knows the neighborhood of basketball. And the two have to mesh. I just have to be the referee once in a while."

Above: "We're in this together..."

Opposite: Coach Brown passes on some wisdom.

Above: Jordan and Jackson—the epitome of a successful player-coach relationship.

that would have sent Iverson to the Los Angeles Clippers, the NBA's version of Siberia, then to Detroit in a four-team, 22-player deal. Iverson was furious and truly shaken.

"I told him that no one I know controls his destiny better than he does," said Croce. "All he has to do is follow Coach Brown's rules and he won't go anywhere. It's that simple."

With Iverson's contract running six years through the 2005 season (worth $70.875 million), something clearly had to give. Brown had been considered for the vacated job at his alma mater, the University of North Carolina, that same summer and despite opting to stay in Philadelphia, had clearly been pushed to his limit by the Iverson saga.

"It's been going on for four years," Brown said of the tension between the two. "Could it be handled better? Probably. Would the results be better?

Probably not.

"Let me put it this way: why should there be a rift between a coach and player if I ask them to be on time to practice like everybody else and lift like everybody else and stretch like everybody else? Why should it be my problem?

"I've been hearing the same conversation about 'I'm going to change and I'm going to do better' for four years. Somewhere along the line, you've got to say, 'Hey, I've got to be responsible enough and care about the team enough.' And I don't know what the answer is there..."

"I wonder what your relationship would be with any employee you might have who doesn't choose to come to work on time, or who doesn't choose to come to work at all, who doesn't choose to do the things everybody else in the organization does, and then says he's upset with the way he's being treated."

Iverson maintained his relationship with Brown was irrelevant. "You don't have to be friends with the coach or even like him," said Iverson. "All you got to do is play and can't nobody say anything bad about my game."

Just the same, Iverson elected to compromise. He came to camp that fall in better shape than he had ever been. He even asked to be captain. And then the two talked.

Iverson said he felt Brown did not respect him, that he judged him by an expression on his face, when, in fact, said Iverson, he intently listened to him. "I want to have the kind of relationship with you," Iverson told Brown, "that Magic Johnson had with Pat Riley and Michael Jordan had with Phil Jackson."

That seemed to do it.

By December 2000, Brown sounded convinced of Iverson's sincerity. "If I'd have known Allen would be like he is today, I don't think anybody would've considered moving him," Brown said. "He's always tried on the basketball court. It's all the other stuff. If I knew that he was going to be on time, that he was going to come prepared to practice each day, that he was going to be respectful of his teammates, there would never have been any [trade] talk."

Both were trying. Iverson passed more and acknowledged Brown's instructions.

Brown smiled more and invited Iverson's input.

"I'm learning to talk to him when I have a problem," Iverson told *Sports Illustrated*, "and he's learning to talk to me. We've both learned a lot about bas-

ketball and life. I know one thing. Coach's voice will never leave my head as long as I live."

Brown said their relationship was simply destined to be a gradual process. "I mean, this is a different animal," Brown told *ESPN Magazine* in March 2001.

"This is a kid who's just so different from any other that's ever been put on this planet, and it just takes time. You'll go through peaks and valleys, and you just have to fight through it. I think, in his own way, he's made unbelievable strides and he's trying real hard. And I think in five years, if I'm still here, I could be saying the same thing. That he's still trying to find himself."

One day after practice late in the season, Iverson was heard telling a van driver about Brown, "Man, I'm going to win this man a ring. He's been in this league all this time and come so close and never got one. His first one gonna be my first one. Can't wait to see his face when I pour that champagne on his head."

Who would have ever thought?

"There are things that still drive you crazy," said Brown at the time. "I've never had a challenge like this, but it's happening in little steps. It's 8,000 times better than it was. I don't judge anymore. I don't look at things so much as right or wrong. I realize now he's not trying to disrespect his teammates or provoke a reaction. It's just the way he is. I keep reminding myself of how he treats his mother and his family. He's got such a big heart. If I were a player, he'd be one of my best friends. It's a joy to see people focusing on the good things. He could do more for the game than anyone because of who he was and how he's changing. It could be the story of what our league is all about."

It could definitely be the story of Brown versus Iverson.

"I think the student taught the teacher a lot about life and I'm grateful for that," Brown said after Iverson's won the NBA's MVP award. "I'm really grateful for the opportunity to coach Allen and I never thought I'd say that."

"I want to have the kind of relationship with you," Iverson told Brown, "that Magic Johnson had with Pat Riley and Michael Jordan had with Phil Jackson."

CAPTAIN IVERSON

Larry Brown had to be laughing inside when his star player made the request. Iverson had asked before and his coach had not hesitated in turning him down.

Captain? Brown was incredulous. How could Iverson possibly think he had the qualifications to be a team captain when he couldn't manage to get to most of their practices on time?

But this time it was going to be different, Iverson said before the start of the 2000–01 season. And this time, Brown believed him.

Iverson was named co-captain with Eric Snow and so began the best season of his career. And not just the best, but the most responsible.

"It just seemed funny for us to have this team and I'm the leader on the floor and not the captain," Iverson said, explaining his reasoning. "People care about what I say and do on the court, and people pay attention to it and a lot of times, they respect it.

"Being captain is a great honor. I'm not the type to talk a whole lot. I just want to be the type of captain who leads by example, plus I don't think a lot of people besides myself think I can handle something like this. I wanted an opportunity to prove I can be a leader, that I can do all the little things to make this team successful."

Brown admitted he was skeptical.

"I had heard a lot of this before," Brown told the *Washington Post*. "The truth is that Allen was usually pretty good in training camp, and then it falls apart when we start playing games. I don't think he ever really understood what it was to be a good teammate. But this time, I figured, it's time. He'd been in the league long enough and he'd been through a lot over the summer."

By November 2000, even those who had been critical of his behavior in the past, were praising their new co-captain.

"The most important thing is that Allen has changed in a lot of ways," said

Above: Iverson's enthusiasm is infectious.

Above: Eric Snow and team-mates now look to Iverson for leadership as well as points.

forward Tyrone Hill. "He's more vocal, not just in practice but in the games."

Teammate George Lynch concurred. "Normally at this point, he would have been late for practice or a meeting," said Lynch. "But he's been on time, attentive, focused on playing. He's been serious. When you see your captain doing everything, you feel you have to do something too.

"That he's willing to accept the responsibility, that's a good thing. He's done everything in my eyes that it takes to be a captain."

Then Sixers president Pat Croce sounded like a proud papa. "I told Allen I was proud of him," Croce said in November. "I told him I'm proud of the way he's playing, proud of the way he's conducting himself, proud of the way he's handled everything after what transpired this summer. It speaks to the kind of person Allen is, the kind of man he has become."

Iverson was actually contrite as he accepted praise for doing things that should have been expected of any player—coming to practice on time, working hard, attending weight-lifting sessions, treating Brown with respect.

"That's the way I should have been the whole time I was here," he

"It's important for me to try and set an example for my teammates to come here and not be fined, and let them see me staying after practice, because then they'll work on their games more."

Above: Iverson and teammates look on during the NBA Finals against the Lakers.

admitted early in the season. "It took a lot of misfortune for me to understand that, but now I do.

"It's important for me to try and set an example for my teammates to come here and not be fined, and let them see me staying after practice, because then they'll work on their games more. I always went off raw talent. Now I'm listening to the coaches more, getting more advice from those guys...staying after, coming early."

Iverson said at the conclusion of the season that all he wanted to be able to do was look himself in the mirror and know that he gave it his best. "That'll be enough for me to walk away from the mirror happy," he said. "I knew, regardless of being the captain, there was going to be a change in Allen Iverson. Not as a player, but as a person. I knew that coming in.

"Coach Brown felt just being Allen Iverson, doing everything the right way, is a good enough captain for him. Doing everything the right way didn't have anything to do with basketball. It was about other things."

Brown could not have been happier about the transformation.

"I've always maintained if the better players lead by example, you can just coach," said Brown. "That's what's fun."

TO THE PROMISED LAND

It was the Monday after the Philadelphia 76ers won the Eastern Conference Championship and Allen Iverson still couldn't believe he was headed to the NBA Finals against the Los Angeles Lakers.

"I can't remember the last time I got up that early smiling as much as I was this morning," Iverson said the day after his best all around game of the series with 44 points, seven assists and six rebounds in the Game 7 victory against the Milwaukee Bucks. "I was so happy. Happy to be alive, happy to be a part of everything. I couldn't wait for the opportunity to get back to the gym, to see my teammates, to talk about their night last night. It feels good."

It was Iverson's first trip to the Finals, the first for his coach, Larry Brown, in 18 seasons, and the first for the Sixers in 18 years as well.

Prognosticators had them finishing in the middle of the Eastern Conference behind Orlando, Miami and New York, at the very least. But buoyed by a more mature Iverson and a supporting cast with a chip on its collective shoulders, the Sixers began the season at 10-0 and never looked back.

By the time they were through, Philadelphia had the best record in the conference and had secured homecourt advantage in the playoffs at least up until the Finals, a major factor in their series victories over Toronto and Milwaukee.

There were, to be sure, setbacks and question marks along the way. When the Sixers traded Theo Ratliff for Dikembe Mutombo, cynics thought it was a mistake. And when George Lynch broke his foot against Toronto, then Eric Snow sustained a stress fracture in his ankle against Milwaukee and finally, Iverson sat out Game 3 against Milwaukee with a bruised tailbone, prevailing wisdom was that the journey would soon be over and the Finals would remain a dream.

"We've been counted out for the longest time," said Aaron McKie. "But we have an agenda and if we don't believe in ourselves, no one else will."

By November, the Sixers knew themselves they were for real. There was the nifty ball movement, the stubborn defense, the overall teamwork and then, there was Iverson.

Shooting less and more judiciously than he ever had in his career, passing more, turning the ball over less, playing smarter and, perhaps most significantly, providing true leadership to his team, Iverson was willing the Sixers to their best season in years. And they were responding.

"I knew it was up to me to do the little things, showing up for practice, being someone my teammates could look up to," Iverson said of the change in him. "For the first time in my life, I sat down and said, 'Look, it's time for me to be a professional and not just a basketball player."

By December, Iverson was shooting just 37 percent, though still having his best all around season while averaging 27 points per game, and that supporting cast, a group of role players who worked hard and knew their place, was more than holding its own. Eric Snow was shooting 54 percent and scoring 20-plus points on a regular basis after managing to top 20 just twice before the 2000–01 season.

"During the [1999] playoffs, I don't think he had that much confidence in the rest of us," teammate George Lynch said in December 2000. "He talked about it, but he still felt he had to make the big shot. You can tell he has matured. Winning games is more important than winning scoring titles."

By early February, the Sixers still had the best record in the league, despite a stretch of injuries, and the ravaged body of Iverson, who played with a sore hip, a bruised elbow, a partially dislocated shoulder, a twisted knee and a sore thigh. Suddenly, the Sixers were looking at a stretch run in which they were being talked about as championship contenders and Iverson was a leading candidate for NBA Most Valuable Player.

But looming ominously ahead were still the Indiana Pacers, the team that had knocked the Sixers out of the playoffs the previous two springs.

Iverson would cry after it was over, the Sixers first-round victors despite his 10-for-31 shooting night. "Tears of joy," said Iverson, who was still the most important player on the floor and still scored 33 points in establishing that traps and double teams aside, no team would shut him down completely.

And no team would, not even the eventual world champion Lakers.

Iverson, favoring a sore hip and as is his customary style, bouncing off bigger players all night, would finish with a game-high 37 points in the final game of the series as the overmatched Sixers would come back from behind time and again, earning a prolonged standing ovation from their crowd despite their defeat.

"I'm just so proud of my team," said Brown. "People need to understand how hurt our guys were...how they never gave up and kept fighting. The NBA Comissioner [David Stern] came by to see me after the game to tell me how proud he was of our guys, how much character they showed. I couldn't agree with him more."

Iverson, as usual, had flashed his trademark bravado before the Finals had begun. "We'll leave our hearts on the floor," he vowed.

No one could argue that he did.

"This team has gotten better every year since Allen has been here," said center Todd MacCulloch. "I would expect next year to be no different."

Opposite: Despite his injuries Iverson played all out against LA.

Above: Iverson's game was too much for the Pacers to handle.

BECOMING A PRO

When Allen Iverson was a rookie, then-NBA star Charles Barkley gave him a nickname. Barkley called him "Me-myself-and-Iverson."

It's safe to say Iverson quickly established a reputation of selfishness, and the veterans of the game were not going to let him shake it for a while.

When Iverson played in his first All-Star game, the NBA honored its 50 greatest stars in a special half-time presentation. When asked specifically about Iverson, former greats like Rick Barry and Elgin Baylor said he wasn't a team player and that he needed to show more respect for the players who came before him.

"He's not the greatest, he's just the latest," Barkley said of Iverson. "Did you see those 50 great players out there at half-time? I don't think Allen Iverson is ever going to be as good as those players."

If Iverson did not take the criticism to heart at the time, it would eventually eat at him. Not making the 2000 Olympic team was a blow and an obvious snub. And after the Sixers nearly traded him, Iverson made a decision.

Before the 2000 season, he made a proclamation to team president Pat Croce. "He said that he screwed up for 24 years in the past, and when he turned 25 in June, he said he wanted to be a professional."

For Iverson, the reasons had nothing to do with improving his public image or gaining more fans. "This is my fifth year and I haven't won a championship," he said. "I don't think I did the things necessary to win it. I had to stop acting like a kid and start doing some extra work. There were a lot of small things Coach Brown wanted me to do that I didn't do and should've never had a problem doing. Now I'm doing them."

Some said Iverson simply had to get some experience to see the error of his ways. As a rookie, perception around the league of Iverson was a player trying to learn and change, but clinging to the wide-open style that got him to that point.

At that point, he was already being called as quick as anyone in the history of the league. He already had his deadly crossover dribble. And he didn't see the need to pass the ball.

> **"This is my fifth year and I haven't won a championship. I don't think I did the things necessary to win it. I had to stop acting like a kid and start doing some extra work."**

Above: Charles Barkley was one of many who were made to eat their words.

In that rookie year under then-coach Johnny Davis, Iverson was urged to shoot and he responded by scoring 40 or more points in five straight games. The Sixers lost all five.

Years later, Iverson said part of the problem were the expectations foisted upon him.

"When I first came into the league, everybody saw the talent God gave me and wanted to make me a guy that was 35 years old," he said. "Nobody ever gave me room for mistakes.

"Everybody felt like since I had the talent that I had, I was supposed to know everything on and off the court when, in actuality, that's not true for anybody. Everybody makes mistakes and everybody gets better. And I'm just getting better on and off the court."

Iverson said he started focusing on people that mattered, his family, coaches and teammates, and did not worry about the perception of him around the league. "Once I start concentrating on everybody else outside of that and trying to make everybody love Allen Iverson, that's when there's going to be a problem. You end up pulling your hair out instead of playing basketball."

During the summer of 2000, Iverson was cryptic with reporters, saying he intended to do something he had never done before. In October, he explained what he meant. "I meant, as far as being a professional, other than just playing basketball," he said. "Doing the little things it takes to make me a better player than I am now. I always relied on raw talent. All I had to do was wake up, come in the gym and be able to play the way I'm capable.

"But it doesn't work that way. Every time you're not working on your game, somebody else is working on their game and getting better. That's a scary thought, watching everybody pass you when you can go so much further than

they can. So I've been spending a lot of time before and after practice trying to sharpen up my game.

"I'm just looking forward to having the best season I've had so far. I don't think that comes with stats or anything like that. It just comes with being the leader, just trying to do the little things that I haven't done, something positive with my body."

Iverson wouldn't limit himself. "Every aspect," he said. "Even trying to get faster. People always say I'm the fastest guy in the league, but I'm even trying to get faster. I'm working on my shot. It's important to get my free throw percentage up and my field goal percentage up, just trying to concentrate on not taking so many bad shots.

"I'm trying to mature in my game, trying to accept that I can get better, stop trying to fight it. Once you make the All-Star team or first-team NBA, that doesn't mean you can't get better. I'm just trying to drill that in my head. Hopefully, if I get better, my teammates will, and hopefully we can win a championship."

Brown said at that point, he was doing everything better: "His overall game is the best since I've been here," said Brown. "I've always said if you play winning basketball, all the other stuff will come. Now to see all the positive stories about him, about the sacrifices he made in his game...He's all about playing the right way."

In May 2001, Iverson set a new team playoff record with his 54 points against Toronto. Asked what was the source of energy that contributed to the evening and it was evident how much Iverson's perspective had changed.

"Life," he replied. "Going through the things I've been through, trying to get to this point. Poverty. Everything. I feel like God gave me an opportunity to do something positive with my life. A lot of guys from my neighborhood would love to be here. Not to score 54 points, but just to be here, on the bench, part of it.

"People always talk about struggling in basketball. There's no struggling in basketball, there's a lot worse. People go through worse things in life every day. To go 0-for-something? I cherish life a little bit more than that."

Above: In his early days as a pro Iverson was sublimely talented but somewhat raw.

Opposite: Iverson's game has continued to mature as Toronto quickly found out.

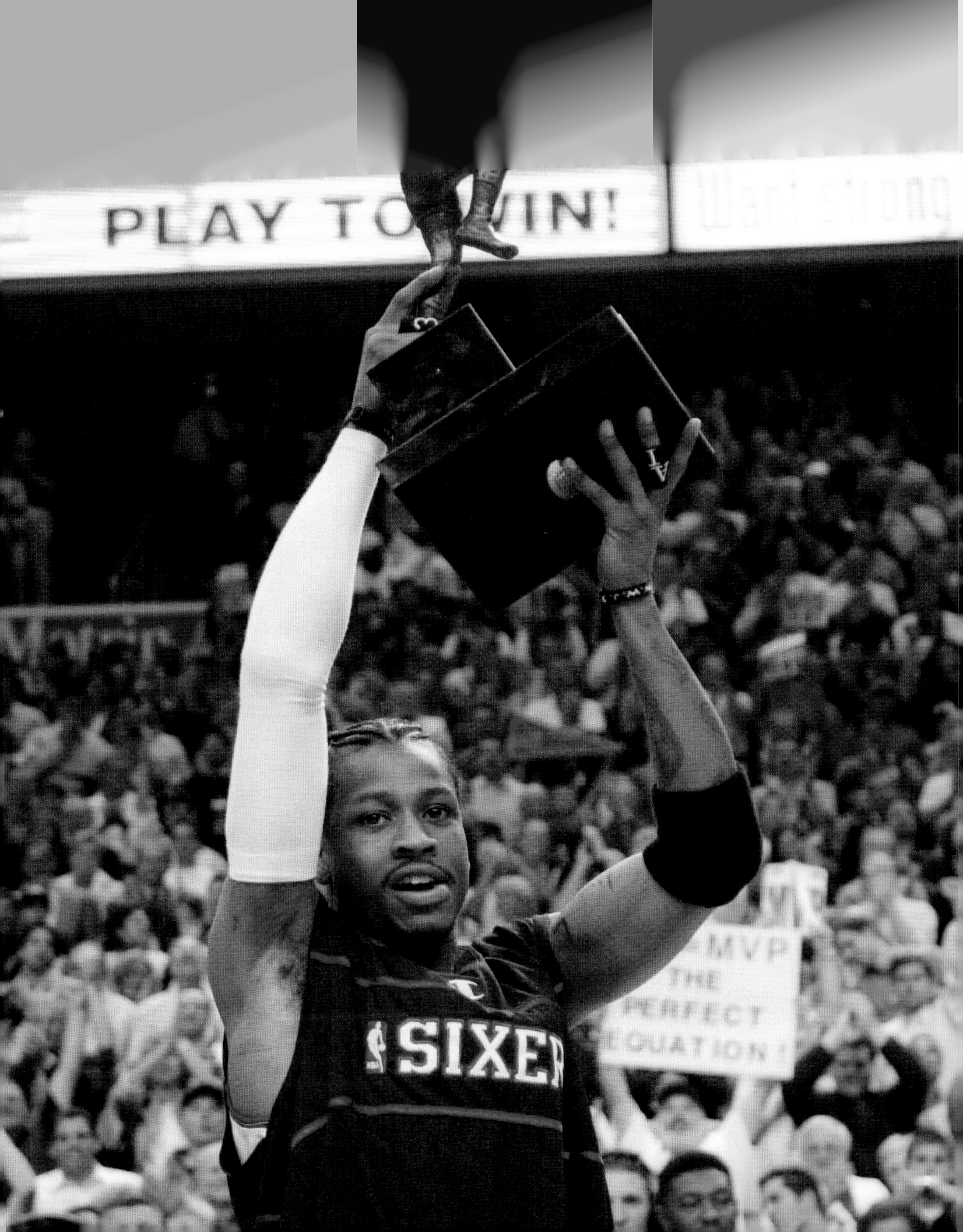
PLAY TO
SIXER
MVP
THE
PERFECT
EQUATION!

"MVP, MVP"

Winning the 1999 NBA scoring title had to give Allen Iverson some satisfaction. It would not, necessarily, however, speak to how valuable he was to his team. And it would not show the rest of the league what he was desperate to prove—that he was truly the best player in the NBA.

Time and again, his coach, Larry Brown, would tell Iverson that if he played the right way, his way, all the accolades he really desired would be his. By November of the 2000–01 season, Iverson could see what he meant.

The Sixers were off to a 10-0 and no one was happier than Brown.

"If you examine it, he's just playing ball," Brown said. "His defense is 100 percent better, his turnovers are down, he's getting rid of the ball sooner and enjoying it more. I hear a couple of jerks in the stands yelling for him to shoot, but the one thing I had always hoped was, once he won the scoring title and made the All-Star team [for the first time in 2000], he'd start to realize all of that is great, but that the bottom line is about winning.

"But you can't convince a player until he buys into the program. I just hope he feels good about what he's doing, because I've had opposing coaches come up to me and say, 'I can't believe what I'm seeing.'"

Despite his relatively diminutive stature, Iverson had improved his rebounding average to nearly five per game and he was consistently leading the Sixers in assists. His shooting percentage improved to over 40 percent, as did his free throw shooting, to 82 percent, and on defense, he was diving for loose balls despite an array of injuries.

Instead of breaking down Brown's plays to create his own shot opportunities, he was now running them and involving his teammates to bring out their best.

"I've seen the change," said forward Tyrone Hill, "and it's still amazing to me."

Iverson would make his MVP charge, breaking out of a mini-slump at mid-season, cementing it at the All-Star game in February.

Opposite: Allen Iverson—MVP!

45

Previous pages: Iverson lit up both the All Star game and the Bucks.

On January 7, he turned in his third 40-plus point game in four outings with a career-high 54 points on 20-for-30 shooting in a four-point victory at Cleveland. The Sixers won all three games in which he scored 40-plus, a far cry from his rookie years, when high-scoring games almost always came at the expense of a victory.

"The most important thing for me now is just to get a win, regardless if I don't play well," he said after the Cleveland game. "As long as I come out with a win, that's what I get satisfaction from."

If that was a turning point in Iverson's season, then the All-Star game was his moment of truth.

In a game not normally known for passionate play or gritty resolve, Iverson scored 25 points, including ten of his team's final 16 and 15 in the final quarter, to lead the East squad to perhaps the most stirring victory in NBA All-Star game history, after which he was named the game's Most Valuable Player.

With his team trailing by 19 points with 10:46 remaining, Iverson gave his team a short pep talk on the bench, then literally carried them to victory.

> "The most important thing for me now is just to get a win, regardless if I don't play well," he said after the Cleveland game. "As long as I come out with a win, that's what I get satisfaction from."

He then scored diplomacy points afterward by paying homage to the game's greats, saying today's players could never take their place.

"I think this will help everyone develop more respect for Allen's game, what he's capable of doing, the impact he's capable of having," said Miami's Alonzo Mourning. "Everybody thinks he's a ball hog and a scorer. But the bottom line is, when he has the ball in his hands, you want the ball in his hands...He continues to amaze me every time he steps on the floor."

Nicknamed "The Answer" before he even went to college, Iverson made his mark with his speed with the ball and it is that attribute for which he is still most respected.

"He's so fast," said teammate Dikembe Mutombo, "it makes it hard for any defender to stop him."

"He so fast," said the Lakers Ron Harper, "I have to rub my eyes."

"He is one of the few players," said former Detroit great Isiah Thomas, "worth the price of admission."

When he scored a new career-high 54 points and a Sixers playoff record in an utterly amazing all around performance in a Game 2 victory against the Toronto Raptors, there was no doubt who was the best player in the league.

"I wish I could find that fountain, that source of energy," said teammate Todd MacCulloch, "and take a drink. He's fueled by his passion."

When Iverson was officially named the NBA's Most Valuable Player on May 14, 2001, it culminated not just his best season in the league, it represented a personal journey from which Iverson emerged, quite literally, a new person.

"I had to look in the mirror and see things I wasn't doing right as a person and as a player," Iverson said. "I promised myself when I looked in the mirror after this season, I'll know I did everything right."

Iverson had 93 first-place votes out of a possible 124 from the panel of sportswriters and broadcasters in the United States and Canada, to edge out San Antonio's Tim Duncan and the 2000 MVP, L.A.'s Shaquille O'Neal.

Below: Isiah Thomas has been suitably impressed by Iverson.